# Through The Dark And To The North Node

By

**Brandi Paxton**

# Dedication

To my spirit guides. Thank you for always showing up on time.

# Acknowledgments

To my ancestors… I feel you near. Thank you for pouring ancient wisdom into me.

Bishop Michael E. Paxton

Jean L. Paxton – Thomas

Angela Y. Boatwright

John L. "Mike" Paxton

Eloyd Thomas

Pastor Ada L. Price

Brother James L. Price

# About the Author

Former corporate American professional, vocalist, scholar, mother, mentor, spiritual advisor, daughter of a bishop and now author, she follows her God-given passion and shares her perspective with the world. Brandi, is a millennial spiritual practitioner, medium and guru now leading people to God. Her provocative approach to common topics is both polarizing and stimulating to society, yet a light in the darkness. This book is a compilation of prayers and messages to the church from a church kid.

# Table of Contents

# Chapter 1

# Dark Feminine

**Dark Feminine**

# To all the people I ever loved

Peace is expensive. It'll cost you full devotion to the pursuance of your highest self. It'll cost you unrequited love. Real love comes with peace. The two should never be confused, but they always are. Love and unrequited love that is. Love sees you and says, *I'll always be true*. Unrequited love says *I'm too busy to be true to you, too*. And that's when you'll know it's time to move along. Sadly, I've had more unrequited love in my life than any other kind of love. And I know I'm not alone in that.

I fall in love easily. It doesn't take much for me to see a soul at its purest and decide to love it, flaws and all. It's the way God made me, and no matter how hard I try to change who I am, I can't. I'm a lover. I'm a mother at my core. I see every soul as a child that's waiting to be loved…a soul seeking care and understanding. Because of that fact, I have laid down and allowed my soul to be trampled on. I have been slapped in the name of "love." I have been raped in the pursuit of love. I have been scapegoated in the name of keeping the peace for the ones I loved. There's not much I haven't or wouldn't do for love. I've traveled thousands of miles for love.

Today, I decided that I would allow love to take a seat on my lap and pour into me all that I've poured into others. The saga ends today. Unrequited love ends today. No more abuse for the sake of pursuing a love I've never known. I said goodbye to family, friends, career, and life as I had known it. I never quite saw that I was the gold in each love scenario. I am the magic in each love scenario because my love is pure. It doesn't come around for the sake of money, sex, or accolades. It sticks around for the long haul, unadulterated.

So, to all the people I ever loved, unrequited. You deserve my absence. You, there with your ego, must've pushed me so far that the levee broke. You must've ripped the chambers of my heart loose in an effort to take EVERYTHING I had. You must've been really dark to want to hurt someone who gave you all she had. Your heart deserves to ooze from your sternum as I call back my love energy into myself. Your soul deserves to seep into the ground as the energy I gave you to live leaves your aura.

What made you this dark? A dollar? My unwillingness to be disrespected by you any longer? What made you curse the day I awakened to your ruse? What made me your enemy? Was it a missed funeral? Was it your own sexual abuse? Was it your own failure to succeed? I gave and gave and gave until you broke me.

May the ancestors bind your negative intentions, thoughts, and words and return them to you with interest.

# Just call me Jezebel, then!

What are we if we aren't our sister's keepers? Some of us are called to this earth to walk a path of love and luxury. Some of us are called here to let our lives be a reflection of God's immeasurable grace. Some of us are called to labor and toil for years while people tell our stories, whether they are true or fables. Often, the story goes on and is never properly told.

All of my life, the name Jezebel has been synonymously known with every dark side of the feminine. Too much lipstick…Jezebel. Too much cleavage…Jezabel. More than two lovers in a lifetime…Jezzy! How has the world made one name synonymous with everything that Anglican society hates? How have we become so lazy and unable to assign any other name to things we do not understand? With the dictionary still growing and scholars still learning, we have certainly developed more words to define what we mean. Right? I can assure you we are not doing our girl, Jezebel, the justice she deserves.

By now, you're aware of just how annoyed I get with assumptions. And the bible has certainly missed the mark on properly telling the stories of the women within. *Consider reading my earlier submission on Mary Magdalene.* Then, consider everything we know about Jezebel. For months, God has had me on a buzzing journey about Jezebel. Admittedly, my life has been so crazy that I kept putting my studies off to work on other pressing topics and issues and solidifying who I am after divorce. I realize now that it was a bit of a trick. I needed to do all the things: get my feelings hurt a few times, lose friends, be pre-judged, and then completely shut down to be able to receive the revelation of Jezebel. This whole time, I thought I was supposed to be purging her from my life should there be any remnants of her. The real revelation was for me to get to know her for who she was, something most of us have never done.

It's definitely something that people don't often do for me. Get to know me, that is. There have been so many assumptions about me because of simply who I present to be. I, standing at 5 feet 2 inches, am curvy, busty, and unafraid to show it. I walk through life very boldly. The southern in me makes me speak to everyone, and I've been known to be a flirt, though many times, I'm just being nice. Women are not usually comfortable with their man being around me, though I have never broken up a happy home or pursued anyone who was not "available." But are men ever really available? At least, emotionally speaking? Amongst the lies and deception that most judgmental people go on carrying, there's usually some lie waiting to be told. Like, how a husband is in love with two men and not his wife. Oftentimes, she's the last to know or the first to want to deflect from the reality of her unfilling life. But let's leave that alone for now.

The revelation God wanted me to see was there were so many things Jezebel and I have or had had in common. She, the daughter of a king, the wife of a king, and a part of a unit of plural love was a powerful woman.

Highly educated and well versed on how to play what would've been considered "a man's game," she ruled one of the two panels of diptych and was eminent for writing letters to assert her dominance. As a woman, she loathed the inability of the men around her to get things done. She was highly respected for her shrewd way of handling business. Over 800 prophets ate from her table through her devotion to the monarchy and Baal (a nature God). She learned the law and found loopholes in it to give Ahab, her husband and king, the land he desired. She is able to bend men to her will because they see and find a need for her leadership and mind. She let nothing stand in her way, not even the prophet Elijah.

I, the daughter of a Bishop, the former wife to a white male in corporate leadership, a highly educated woman, and a former member of a plural love unit, have been considered in many circles to be well-bred and highly sought after. I have been an adviser to businessmen, and I have been able to will my way through scholarship, career, and strategy into some of the best places in life. I have stayed at some of the best hotels and eaten some of the finest meals for free because…strategy. Very determined to win, I let nothing stand in my way. I have been known to write a letter or two to get things done as I desired (something I give my grandmother credit for; she could write a sharp nastygram, pen to paper). Focused on living the life I wanted to live, I pushed my ex-husband to heights he never imagined (his words). Well-versed in church culture and business culture and pretty experienced in street culture, I have been able to marry knowledge and wisdom to ascend to places I never thought were open to a black woman. Yes, there is a privilege that comes from being a bishop's daughter. There is much more benefit from being the wife of a white man in Middle America. I played the role and well, at that. And my moniker alone shows how powerful I believe that I am (brag, not humbly).

Both Jezebel and I have had our names become synonymous with dark feminine. I have been called a Jezebel before, actually. I say, if free agency makes me a Jezabel, then so be it! The problem in society today is that people are afraid to be themselves for fear that others may judge them. People cower at the possibility that, just maybe, there is more to be had in life. They worry about a woman at the helm of any sort of leadership, let alone a black woman. They worry when a woman asks for sex, talks about pleasure, and dares to tell a man no. They worry when a woman dares to exude the confidence she's earned from having been a victim of her circumstance, then posturing that victimhood into victory and confidence.

They go into utter chills when a woman takes the mystique off of taboo topics in hopes of encouraging other women to be who they are. And as Jezebel worshipped the monarchy and Baal (and possibly Asherah, a cult), I'd venture to say that the Christian faith and the Catholic Church have done a number on the planet when it comes to mini-functioning cults across the globes hidden under the guise of denomination and organization. That used to be me, a cult member, though many would never agree that an apostolic church in the mid-south that was prohibited from wearing anything that remotely showed skin or feet was a cult. The moment I publicly said I was a "spiritualist," people lost their shit! How dare she? What would her father think? What does her mother, the pastor, think? What would her grandmother, the first black female pastor in Wisconsin, think if she were alive? The pearls have been clutched so much that the strings are being used to proverbially hang church members across the globe in abhorrence to my personal reverence of God versus religion. Jezebel's own people killed her in a push to her death. It is likely that my own would do the same if they could get close enough to me. I admit I'd fix my eyeliner and reapply my lipstick, just as Jezzy did before the dogs tore my flesh. My grandmother would be mortified if I started my journey to the afterlife without a good application of makeup.

Like Jezzy, people don't usually get to know me before passing judgment. I have deduced that it's because, to my southern friends and family and religious fanatic acquaintances, I am too loud, too proud, and too on-purpose with my mission(s) in life. I don't mind trying many things to see if something sticks. I don't mind looking like a fool in my attempt to liberate myself. I am cool with being disliked, and I keep receipts. I *am* loyal! Until you show me that I should *not* be. And until recently, I would go down fighting for everyone I loved. And that is where Jezebel's downfall lies, in my opinion. She was too loyal to the monarch, her king, and her God. She did not have the foresight or spiritual wisdom to see how history would commemorate her. She could not see the torrential downpour of hate that would come and never stop flooding when an unbeloved woman was spoken of. She thought her loyalty would keep her in the special graces of everyone who served her and whom she served. It did not. And mine will not either.

Her husband, the king, preceded her death and could not save her. Her two sons, both kings, preceded her in death; they could not save her, either.

Her countryman turned on her and ultimately, her story ends as her being the worst possible human on the planet and one of the worst references of a woman to ever exist. The Bible never referenced her as a queen or a ruler, though she was one. The Bible never referenced her as a visionary, but that she was. The bible never referenced her as a change agent. And really, there are women in churches everywhere that are fully covered, bible-toting, and have half of the truth that she did. There are women clergy that sleep with hundreds of men in a lifetime, but since they lie about it, they are hailed as some of the greatest orators of our time. And as there was no reference to her being a sexual deviant or expositionist, there isn't much reason to associate her with sex, though her husband had many wives and children while they were wed. She was clearly the brains of the operations, though the bible categorizes her as a manipulator. Ha! Show me a pretty woman with curves, and then tell me how she can't manipulate anyone at all. Maybe Bathsheba could chime in? In fact, show me a woman who hasn't used her feminine wiles to get an extra gift from her husband year after year. I think Jezebel's significance was that she was publicly powerful and unapologetic.

The revelation here is that we, women, are all Jezabel unless cowardice and mediocrity are your fulfillment in life. So, call me Jezebal. I'm fine with it, really. And since there isn't a man or woman alive that can tell you just how many people I have bedded, you can let it rest with the assumptions. The concern for my sexual adventures far outweighs the concerns for my sexual assaults, and *that* is sick! No need to cry for me; I have healed. But if you are tuned in, you will see that my mission is not to have sex with every person on the planet; it is to get people to wake up! And that is not limited to gender, either. Am I perfect? It depends on who you ask. Am I intentional? Yes. Am I fervent in my spiritual mission and life purpose? Absolutely!

Perhaps people should turn the light inward and check their audacity. You may not like Jezebel, but she did things very few women could. She did the things even men of her time couldn't. She used what she had to get what she desired. Fortunately for her, she was beautiful, smart, creative and strategic. Let history remember her for that, as well.

Hermitly, I have been navigating a path to spiritual ascension and freedom. This, a journey I could not do while wed, has become a great way for me to see who is in my corner. It has helped me skim the crowd for clout chasers and off board silent enemies. Unlike Jezabel, I have the spiritual gifts of foresight, wisdom, and cojones to be who I am in 2024. You know who really hates that? Women. They walk through my social media profiles with what seems like red pins to point out my flaws and call me a fake. A fake what, really? I'm not a preacher. Though, I am ordained to marry people (if you're interested, reach out to me). I have publicly displayed my flaws and my healing process and told everyone exactly who I was. So, what about me is fake? Or is it that people are so used to lies that the truth is too uncomfortable?

As a person in an endless life of healing, I beg of our society to work on self. We cannot condemn strong women for their strength. We should not condemn women for their darkness, lest we remember Lillith and understand her. True self-discovery is understanding our darkness and learning how to bend it to our will.

If anything bad shall be said about Jezebel, let it be that she was controlling, a thief, a liar, and a bad prophet. Or, we can just call her a politician. Or maybe we should call her mom, as many of us have learned to work a room and be manipulative from our mothers. While we are on the journey to cleanse ourselves of the evil parts of Jezebel, let us remember her strength and familiarity. Or rather, let her die. She's long since held the gaze of judgmental humans. Let's birth *new* women.

# Chapter 2

# South Node

# "Hello, God! Is Weed Bad?"

I'm a machine when I'm passionate about something. The hardest part for me is finding fewer things to be passionate about, honestly. I care about everything and everyone, it seems. It's been an Achilles heel for me throughout life. I'd like to think I learned to be this way by watching so many people in my life pursue their dreams and aspirations. But I think it's who I am. It's who I was born to be. Religion is one subject that has caused me to pause on the regular, though.

I was raised Pentecostal, and that lens of God can be very limiting. Over the course of my life, I have learned to seek God for direction and allow him to guide me on what is truly right and wrong as it relates to my relationship with The Divine. It's really the only way I can make sense of the chaos that I've watched happen in churches across the US. The hypocrisy is incredibly discouraging, or it can be. It's much less of a burden for me now because I am on my purpose and on a daily mission to keep going toward my North Node. That sentence alone shows the complexity of what I believe to be true for me. It's certainly nothing you'd hear in most southern Pentecostal black churches.

I am a chronic pain survivor. I have been in pain for most of my adult life, and as life would have it, pain increases over age/injury. In 2018, my doctor looked at me and gave very illegal advice on how to get marijuana to microdose it for pain. LOL! He also followed it up with information on how to do it legally. A few months later, I was licensed and paying the ungodly amount that is medical marijuana tax in a state that isn't recreational. It's really ridiculous what they do to folks with taxation on something you can get for much less from an old lady growing a plant in her attic or your cousin's friend who's been a dime-bag seller for years. Now, the product is legal to consume here in Ohio. Of course, that doesn't mean that you can consume it and use it after work. Companies do still have policies for that, and for good reason, which is one of the benefits of not being on anyone's payroll.

Was marijuana helpful for my pain? Yes. I struggled with using it regularly because of my religious upbringing. And then, pain at 4 a.m. starts to change your tone. I found out what my limits were and stuck within them. I think that's the responsible thing to do. Start low and see what you can tolerate. I don't think it's for everyone, though. When I started drawing closer to God and seeking him for guidance, I decided to stop using it altogether. All praise to God for that one. I just didn't need to use it. Almost six months, spliff-free! And then, recently…pain. I took one toke one day, and during that euphoria, I prayed and asked God for guidance on whether this was really a "sin." Is this something that I should be ashamed of? Am I somehow working against the flow of God by using this medicine, as prescribed by my doctor? Does having it prescribed by a doctor matter? What is the big deal?

"God, show me!"

The message I received (once sober) was about temperance and the chemicals being put into the product. And, of course, vocals…I AM a singer, so I should certainly be concerned about that. **What is the church's stance on marijuana?** I often think of my father, a bishop, who sadly lost his battle with metastatic cancer. The pain, I'm told, that he was in must have been a reason for him to release his will to God in exchange for death. Is God really concerned about marijuana? Is God concerned about a 64-year-old man dying of cancer and taking a toke or two in order to achieve relief? What about a perfectly healthy person who chooses to have an edible on the weekend to induce relaxation? In the landscape of God's plan, is he hung up on who is safely using marijuana? I'm assuming churches are either avoiding the subject or damning it to hell, but perhaps I'm wrong.

Are churches the authority on what humans should consume? What about alcohol? Every Catholic person I know drinks wine. Every Pentecostal I know that drinks wine lies about it. I know many Pentecostals. I know many of them that drink alcohol. Why is that? Why have we become so comfortable with condemning ourselves based on the opinions of another person? Or a book that's been rewritten, chopped, and screwed at least a dozen times or in different ways? Have we become so comfortable with condemnation that we won't even allow ourselves the opportunity to seek God for direction on what is best for our lives? What are we teaching our children by living double lives? What are we telling God (as though he isn't watching) when we lie to others about our consumption?

Clearly, I'm not the authority on what's right or wrong. I think we should allow our relationships with God to be the compass for us and ensure that we are tempered and safe when consuming marijuana and alcohol. I'm no prude, but I certainly am out of practice on one of the day-long wine tours my girlfriends and I have done. I believe that my discernment will guide me on when enough is enough, just as it did for the wedding goers in Cana in John 2:1–12.

I care. I sincerely want to do and be right with all of the universe. I always have. I'm just made that way. I really, really care about people. My pivot into the veil of The Divine has me questioning all things on the matter of the soul and not just my own. I find that all matters in my life; education, talent acquisitions, philanthropy, and even my old job at Radio Shack, have made me into the being I am. I understand people and human nature. Real time connection is not just important in the classroom. It's important in the pews of the sanctuary, as well. It is incumbent upon church(es) to be concerned as well. Ministering to souls means ministering to the whole person, which may require putting the Bible down and discussing topics like these.

First, natural, then spiritual, right.

# Waging War on Under-Education: The Church

A good word spreads far and wide and has the ability to single-handedly change lives. Storytelling is one of the earliest forms of education. How we tell stories now is drastically different, but no less important in the information age. So many people rely on gossip sites, satirical pages, and even celebrities for their news, negating real journalistic work and rigor in fact-checking. These days, if it's on *Facebook*, it's law. And that is a problem! We've stopped thinking for ourselves, stopped asking questions, and quite frankly, we've shamed people into believing that if they don't immediately grasp something, they are, in some way, null. We've shamed people into silence. Listen, I'm sure I've done it too. There's no doubt that in one of my soapbox moments, I've alienated someone amidst the ten-dollar college words I'm still paying for.

But that has to change. It's time we re-educate America and adults across the globe, though we really need to spend the extent of our time on Americans. We have a real problem with learning deficits in America, much more widespread than we have data to support. Why is this? See healthcare, systemic stigmas with diagnoses, the significant mental health crisis in America, our failing education system, the internet, and the parental gap dating as far back as the "latchkey" era, just to name a few. Maybe just scroll through social media during an election cycle. Our adults are so undereducated in a country with an absorbent amount of education debt. There is no wonder why our children are falling so far behind.

In Acts 8 of the Bible, we are introduced to Philip the Evangelist, who was led by an angel towards goodwill and purpose. Educated, a eunuch was sitting in a chariot reading the works of Isaiah aloud. Philip, led by the direction of an angel, ran over to inquire if the eunuch knew what he was reading. The eunuch's response is, "How can I unless someone teaches me."

Now, some would assume that because he could read, he might be able to comprehend. But that is just the same issue we have today. People can read (*insert happy ADOS emoji*), but they struggle to comprehend what is being grasped. Even in religious-based settings, the doctrine is being taught based on one person's understanding or revelation of a word. Many end up living their whole lives believing scriptural texts mean something it does not, or they misunderstand the benefit of time periods and circumstances in texts. With the intimidation of digesting revered texts, many avoid it altogether. The same is true of other works of literary art.

Philip went on to educate the eunuch on what he was reading and who Jesus was. The eunuch accepted Christ into his life and was baptized that very day. That is the power of education and faith coming together! It's time we relaunch the mission.

We need to start over. We need to re-educate the adult and watch how that changes the education of the child, the workplace, the community, and even our voting stances. People are ignorant! With as much information available to us, we are still stumbling upon the banks of illiteracy. A sad truth.

I propose we start the reeducation of America in churches. A safe place. A place receiving the benefit of tax-free status. A local place in every neighborhood. Teaching regular reading and writing, not doctrine. If we can educate people to understand concepts, people will much better understand a doctrine that fits their lives, which is the way any great deity would want it. Free will and faith are coming together to start the largest revolution of our time.

Open the doors of the church to not only souls but to education, regardless of belief!

*ADOS: American Descendant of Slavery

**South Node**

# Finding God, for real: Finding the Signal and getting "the call."

I know God is real. All my life, I've searched for Him. I looked for Him in music. He was there. I journeyed through life and found Him in pain. I took the scenic route through education and careers, and He was most definitely there. But it was only when I felt my loneliest when my father died did I find Him, for real. I found Him in the trees, I found Him in the grass…I found Him in sadness, too. One day, it occurred to me that He was with my father. It occurred to me that I was with my father, even in his death. He was near me. Then, I realized that God is everywhere, in everything, and with everyone. There is no denomination in God's eyes. There is only love.

There is no color in God's eyes, only offspring of Himself. There is no small deed in God's eyes, only tasks we were given in order to keep the flow of abundance in rotation. I found God in the craziest of places. I found him in a thug who looked out for me like the most loving father. I found him in a Michigan man who spoke about God's wrath while he committed sins of his own. I found Him in a fifty-something engineer who told me to trust myself. I found Him in heartbreak. I found Him in betrayal. God is definitely out here working hard.

I found Him in the memory of my ancestors and loved ones who have walked their last mile on earth. I found Him, for real, this time. I see Him in the deer in my yard. Or, my old backyard, that is. I found God in a divorce recently (insert shrug emoji). I see Him in the dragonflies that swarm my head when I'm grounding myself. I see Him in the bad decisions I've made. I even see Him in the good decisions that hurt like hell. He's never left me. On my own quest to understand who He really was, I took many roads and wasted a lot of my time seeking validation from people who weren't half as loving or kind as I was. And then, one day, it hit me.

I decided to answer the call that had been coming in for decades. I finally took the phone off DND and answered the call. Once I did that, He showed me my purpose over a series of years. So deep in my misery, I tried to negotiate with God on how to fully execute "the plan" and keep all of "my stuff." I wanted to do the work as fervently but gently as possible. I enjoyed the comforts of my unrenovated home, still nicer than many others' homes though. I found comfort in my luxury car, my dysfunctional marriage, and my weirdly fun teenager. Yes, God was there, too. It was only when I started having more *different* (unlike the ones I've experienced since childhood) supernatural experiences that I realized I had to make changes. I was exhausted with stagnancy.

I started to see that the adversary was also there, too. Like, for real. I started to understand just how spiritual wickedness works. I started to understand that I had been in a fog for decades, on autopilot. I was still the same woman, but I had allowed myself to be taken over by something else. Another entity, while I fought hard to be myself, had nestled its way right into my lap and taken residence. Fighting hard to unearth and debunk the grips of control, deceit, and heartbreak, I started reaching out to my ancestors for guidance. I needed familiar help. Trapped in a marriage I hated but was so used to, I begged God for guidance on how to get out.

Over and over, I asked my father to show up. "Help me" rang out of my soul over and over again. Over and over again, I begged for guidance. And then, one night, like a spiritual band of angels, a force of energy propped me up as my knees knocked and my voice shook as I asked for a divorce for one last time.

And then, I got to see just how close God was. I got to see just how long he'd been there, waiting for me to pull the plug on my own misery. He's been waiting for me to say **when**. He'd been waiting for me to get serious about my liberation. Once I was, He did his thing. He gave me a song to keep singing. I sang it all the way to my divorce attorney. I sang it all the way back to my car. I sang it before our hearing with the judge, and today, I see why this song was mine. Every step of the way, God has made me trust in Him. There's never been in any family for me to rely on. But God showed me how my ancestors had been behind the scenes, too. He showed me, in dreams, how they were working with me. He showed me how they'd always been rooting for my success.

The God I knew before was much less loving. The God I know now is much more sophisticated and authentic. Finally, one thing off my list of things to be an SME (Subject Matter Expert). Mission accomplished.

For all of the PKs (preacher's kid(s)) trying to figure out their own journey with God.

# Chapter 3

# Space

# Understanding the assignment: A Philippians 1:6 ongoing mission

I've been using the moniker Brandi Paxton for a while now. I didn't realize that all that I needed, all that I was seeking, I already had. Outside of it just flowing with my name, history, and swift roll of the tongue, it really feels like it's who I am. Over many months, God has walked me through the gifts that I stopped using, didn't know I had, or the weird quirks that I didn't understand to help me see that I have been on high vibrational thinking for much longer than I realized. And then, I discovered my Lilith and things started to smooth out like butter. I found my darkness and got to know her.

Once I understood the darkest part of who I was, I started to embrace the lightest parts. I also started to understand that God is in all things, even in hell. I started to understand that I needed to embrace the hell in my life in order to grasp the magnitude of the heaven I was experiencing almost daily. I really have been blessed. I've done things, studied things and experienced things that many people may never, simply because of their fear. If God is within me, why would I be afraid? Studying taboo subjects and treading waters other people are fearful of is and has always been fuel for me. Human nature is truly stimulating to me. I've embalmed bodies; I've studied sex; I've studied religion; I've studied education; human behavior; women's health and reproductive disorders; law; systemic bias; labor and employment; history reversal, and so many other things. I have been going through life collecting knowledge and sharing it here and there. I really have done a lot in 39 years. Special mention to having been married to the most powerful species in the world, the white male (and its ego). Yeah, that's a subject that is a giving tree. There are always new lessons and ways to digest that level of privilege. I'm grateful for it as it has been the best and most thorough education of all.

Privilege is inspiring. It makes you want to know things that you shouldn't, and as a black woman, it has been the battery in my back pushing me to try everything. Why not, right? My ex-husband's grandfather opened my eyes to a world that I had never known. He really pushed the gas on, doing whatever it was that I thought I could not. He, standing at six feet, five inches, spoke in a Jim Crow southern privileged white male dialect and demanded everything he wanted from life and everyone within it. He taught me the game. He gave me permission to ask for what I wanted and to fight until I got it. I owe a multitude of thanks to him for his knowledge, his haughtiness, and his racism. Refusing to even sit by me upon our first meeting, he let me know that I was in deep waters that had not been tread by anyone I'd known. Has anyone in my lineage been that close to "the man"? Had anyone been that close to Jim Crow? Had anyone in my family been that close to evil? He scared me, woke me up, and required me to spar with him. Something in me stretched, stared him in the eye, and beckoned him towards me.

The surprise I got with him was annoyingly shocking. In his eyes, he showed his own shock. And he was constantly shocked by my willingness to be myself. I refused to cower. I refused to bow down. I required that he come up from the depths of hell to get his own lessons. At less than five feet and no more than twenty-two years old, talking to me became one of his favorite pastimes. I imagine he rose daily and plotted the things he'd teach me that day. His shock was only to realize that I was the teacher and that the Negroes he'd once tortured as they raised and nurtured him were not the same Negro he was encountering then. He fell in love. Or maybe he developed a new fetish. He started to visit me almost daily and spoke perverse and twisted rhetoric to me to either scare or shock me. What he received was black momma chastisement of epic proportions. I think he wanted it. The more I fought his energy, the more he respected me. Then, he started introducing me as his granddaughter, taking me to lunch, and inviting me to social events. He got more than he bargained for and I do believe he was glad at that fact.

As a former hobby photographer, he gave me direction on how to capture life. He photographed me over and over and showed me my own beauty with the dozens of cameras that were all across his senior living apartment. And then, he showed me the game of life and how to play it as a white man. He died shortly after the birth of my son. His final words to me were a request to "help the dummies." He was concerned that his family wouldn't be able to handle his impending death, and he knew I'd get the job done.

When the time came, I did my part.

I now know that God has had me on assignment my entire life. Every exchange, every friendship, every client, every company, every situation has been an assignment for me to wake the world to its own shadow. It's been my job to reflect back to people who they are and what they are giving out. My teacher? My son. Somehow, I feel he's an ancestor who came long before my father, grandmother, or anyone in my bloodline who traversed America. He's an ancient teacher with wise and poignant words and one-liners that both kill and chill. He's a special gift to this planet.

Everyone who knows him sees it. And so, my assignments continue.

In the last ten months or so, God has given me tasks to complete. Seemingly self-serving, I shuddered at the thought of finally giving the proverbial middle finger to the world in an effort to purge myself from the horrible programming I had been given and to clear my name from the ruthless lies that had been told about me. I was called to live in my Lilith for a while. Channeling Mary Magdalene and Jezebel was the blueprint for navigating a thoroughly painful divorce, industry blackballing, and the horrible reality that I was alone. Sexual abuse and the confusion that comes from such led me into a twenty-year detour. I realize that the detour wasn't, of course; it was Special Forces training, if you will. That time was set aside for me to get my ass kicked and learn how to fight spiritually. I've fought physically before. I do not like that part of myself. Fighting mentally was second nature to me. As spiritual beings, we forget that the physical is the weakest dimension of all. The spiritual atmosphere is where the power lies. The things unseen are where God's mercy derives.

I said some things, made some videos and sang some songs. Did all the things He told me. I stripped down, as he said. Got back to the barest form of who I was and laid myself bare. Nobody liked it. None of my friends really supported it (save Jackie, the fan club of one; I know she just wanted me to feel supported by **someone**). Though they were all aware of the pain I had been suffering for years, no one checked in. Even my oldest and dearest took to their corners of the world while I was, many days, in fear of my life. Just in time, God gave me a new circle of friends to uphold me in prayer (*The Dames* go hard). Still, I continued doing what I was led to do. The spiritual fight was materializing in the physical. I was ill for many days. Not being able to quite articulate how I knew what I knew or why I was responding in such a way, I just continued to allow people to think I was crazy. Nothing new to me in that regard. After all, *I am* a creative.

We're all a little weird. Add in the spiritual elements and you've got an outwardly hot mess.

It was a spring and summer of God taking me into deep meditative states to show me the plots and plans of dear friends to assassinate my character. He let me relive the many betrayals of my family. Almost daily, my gifts were strengthening. My classes were going bananas! He led me to places to do work. He led me to spiritual leaders to learn what I was experiencing. He led me to people who were or had experienced the same things I was experiencing. I became life partners with loneliness as I was urged, led, and, some days, pulled away from people who I had known as solid people in my life. The angel would come before the tower every time. I'd get a warning and then an unveiling of the truth after I followed His lead. But no matter how crazy I knew it'd make me look, I just kept obeying the leading He was giving me.

He led me into another realm of the spirit. Almost like bait, he dangled me across the internet to pass messages to "the church." I see that it was their response that I needed to see. He wanted me to see just how big people's faith was and how small their minds were. It hurt. Real bad. And then he let me see just how much people loved me. They did not. Imagine the painful realization that the people you've prayed fervently for, the people you have financially helped, the people you have shown

# Space

unadulterated love for, did not feel the same for you. Whew! Reality check. As I asked God why, He made me wipe my tears and keep climbing the hills of Ohio. In and out of the woods and trails, I cried out for guidance. I cried out for help. It only made me trust Him more. He was all I had left. Still, I kept trusting him. A Job 13:15 seriousness.

My ancestors came to me in dreams and showed me things that caused deep sadness, breathless tears, and cleared illusions I had known my whole life. Suddenly, I was forced to believe nothing and no one but God and myself. The wisest decision I've made. Once I started to see my own strength, my own purpose, and my own power, my tears turned into triumph. Like daily instruction, He laid out what was to come. He showed me impending deaths. He showed storms, hurricanes, and tornadoes before they happened. He led me to post. It was John 4:48 being laid before me.

People still didn't believe me. Some never will. I now know that many of the things I posted (dreams) have already happened. Some, he's saving for later, I guess. Hey, I just work here! Many of the things I did not post are parts of bigger events, stories and ruses still in play. But that assignment, for me, is over.

Quickly, He shifted me from one thing to the next. Spiritually, I envisioned a stage manager snatching a performer from one scene to the end of a play. Oftentimes, I wasn't allowed to "finish" the thing I was working on. Or so I thought. Sometimes, just as I moved on to the next thing, the thing I was working on before would blow up. Then, I'd see why he didn't let me stay. I started to see why He never let me stay anywhere for too long. Not a job, a man, a friend, a city, a home, a social group…***nothing*** has held onto me for long, though I may have wanted to. For years, I thought it was me. I thought it was because I was doing something wrong. But I learned it was because I was willing to do something right. I was willing to listen to God and my instincts, even if it made me look unhinged. I've never spent much time trying to be anyone's favorite, so the opinion of others doesn't linger with me for long.

# Space

Today, I realize that I'm not for the weak. Nah, you have to have faith and loyalty of epic proportions to *get* me. So, I will likely be alone in this season of my life, a thing I am comfortable with now. But, when He sends my hierophant... The demons we will slay, the love we will make, the nations that will be born... May earth and heaven prepare us both for that day.

On assignment with purpose AND power.

Brandi Paxton, your spirit medium.

**Space**

# "Hello, Brandi! See my response within."

# ~God

I heard back on that question about weed. In fact, I heard back a while ago; I think I just needed to test the theory God was giving me. I believe that we always know the answers to questions we have, especially if we're prayerful. Sometimes, it's just much easier to lay low and ignore the answer. It's really just laziness. Changing a thought process is hard to do. And once you've done all the work to do the opposite of what you're being led to do, why change, right? Wrong. Honestly, I just didn't like the answer I received.

The truth is, I like being lazy. There is so much comfort in laying "in-da-couch" when you've had a painfully hard day. There can be so much pleasure in taking a good bath, toking herbs, and listening to Sade in a room full of lit candles. In goes a glass of Malbec, and zoooooooommmm... No more pain, no more struggle, for that moment. I think our society is enjoying this zoom more and more as marijuana laws change. If only we could reform the laws and release the men and women in prison who have suffered the consequences of their past actions when it was illegal to use marijuana. But that's a story for another day, by another creative, perhaps.

The problem for me is I come from a family with addictive personalities. We are bad at keeping balance. Across one side of my family, their drug of choice is religion. They OD on it and blame others for not joining their binge session. On another side of my family, they are more transparent about their addictions. It's evident in the deaths that we experienced because of the use of drugs and alcohol. And then, there's this middle section. It's a blend of religious fanatics, alcoholics, and cool kids. The common thread? Untruths. Or, some may call them lies.

This former group is particularly interesting because they get the same treatment from the public. It's usually some level of adoration because they "look the part." They either have some version of a mild appearance, ensuring not to over-offend or cause too much attention. Some hide their flasks in their purses, bosoms, or maybe their church hats. Okay, maybe I'm exaggerating a bit on that last part, but I wouldn't be shocked if it were true. As long as they throw in a "glory hallelujah," all is well. But, the addictive gene is lying just beneath the surface, waiting for them to have a bad day.

And I realize that I am just like them. My addictive gene is waiting for me to just tap out of the fight to stay out of the fray. Admittedly, I've had a bad trip or two. I mean, have you tried the edibles in Colorado? Jeeezus! California? I won't even go into detail about the bad trip I had in San Diego. It's too embarrassing to talk about. But, just think about 50 mg of edibles at once, on accident. I was not prepared, especially since it had been years since I'd indulged before that incident. The usual 50mg that normal users can handle was a trip to hell for me.

Don't get me wrong; I know how to microdose and live a functional life to manage pain and anxiety. I just think it's not the way for me. The answer to my previous question to God came in the form of a very common sense spiritual dialogue. I imagine He was a parent looking at me, asking very simple questions.

***Imagine Him asking me these things while wearing a sweater vest.***

*Do you like how you feel when you're high?*

*Do you like tripping out?*

*Do you enjoy how your vocal cords sound when you smoke?*

*Do you like being out of control of your ability to focus? Even if your focus is just a little off?*

*What if you have to randomly take a drug test for something? Do you like that level of anxiety?*

*Do you know what chemicals they are putting in this weed these days?*

# Space

*Do you trust the government to regulate anything?*

My answer to every question was a resounding "no."

And then, I noticed how easily I'd get used to micro-dosing. I noticed how weed could help me rest but also have me hovering over the edge of comatose and catatonic if I wasn't careful. That can be a slippery slope for people with addictive personalities. The further I elevate spiritually, I notice that I experience other effects while high. It's no fun. So, the problem was solved for me. I had my answer. So, I stopped. Cold turkey.

I started to realize that I am one of the lucky ones. I am one of the ones who can manage and control my dosage and stop when I want to. Not everyone is able to do that. Some people need a little help to stop. Some people need a lot of help to stop. A person I love made the brave decision to stop today. A combination of marijuana and alcohol has been consuming their life, and today, they decided to get the help they needed. God reminded me today of this answer he'd given me a while ago.

Is weed bad? For me, it is.

If you or someone you know is struggling with addiction, text 988 from your cell phone for help gaining and navigating your sobriety.

Space

# Yo, God! If you're saying I'm a Luciferian, you might be onto something...

Sitting at my desk writing about legal, religious discrimination, the word Luciferianism came to me. Knowing it had nothing to do with what I was writing, I knew it must've been God. Immediately, I wrote it down to review later. Then, I prayed because...what?! Lucifer? I am not your typical millennial. I don't do scary movies, I don't play with paranormal stuff, and I was not familiar with why I was being given this word. I knew very little about the Luciferians, but I knew that God was calling me to learn. So, I did. Over many months, I reviewed the topic, talked with scholars about it, and read about it. Almost upon a first glance, I knew...

"God, are you saying I'm a Luciferian?" I kept asking over and over again as I learned about what they were, who they were, and what they believed upon inception. I knew there was something I was being instructed to learn. I felt like I was reading a synopsis of many of the things I believe as a person who has grown up in severe Christianity. And yes, severe, as in beyond casual and more than devout. People of the apostolic faith are Radicals. Cultist, if you will. They are exceptionally in touch with hell and not as familiar with heaven, as everything is seemingly the devil. I respect the doctrine, though I have always been certain that it did not align with who I *was*. And as a person who tends to rebel against societal norms that do not make sense to me, I know it is not who I *am*. I am an educator. I like to learn and then teach...everyone...everywhere I can. There's far too much knowledge available for us to blindly believe anything.

## What do Luciferians believe?

Not a religion, but a belief system, Luciferianism at inception suggests that humans should have the right to choose. They should not be forced, scared, or thrust into any belief system that suggests that a deity should rule who they are and how they behave. They believe that humans should be free to act and free to unequivocally accept the consequences of their actions.

Luciferians believe that you should strive for success and wealth and be comfortable with it. Contrary to Christian doctrine, pleasure is not bad, as a Luciferian. There is no need to treat humans any better than they deserve (this is one of my favorites), and humans should get what they give.

While they do encourage kindness, if you are an asshole, you should be treated as such. Period. No niceties are given because of status or social structure.

They also believe that it isn't up to them to convert anyone to their belief system. They respect everyone's beliefs, even though they may disagree with said beliefs. Autonomy is more important than the number of followers they obtain (now, this I can really get with). They do not seek fellowship for fellowship's sake. They genuinely want people to be self-starters and faithful to their call. They do not wish to have "hangers-on."

They believe that we need to do our part on the earth instead of devouring it. How arrogant of humans to want to destroy something given to us to sustain us. As a person with all three earth signs being the top 3 in my birth chart, I feel deeply about this one. My connection to the earth is religion to me. The earth equals God. You cannot have one without the other.

They believe that art and science are both equally relevant and important to human advancement. They both are an absolute must in maintaining the order and stability of human life. When I heard this part, my ears perked up a bit. Imagine living in a society that loves the arts but subscribes to the belief system that science is unimportant. Think COVID-19 and the presidential response to WHO, CDC, Dr. Fauci and others heavily rooted in scientific studies.

They do not believe in the suffering of today for promises of future reward. All you have is today. Think, a twelve step program and the ideology of sober living. This stresses the importance of doing the right thing every day and living in the very moment you are in - a constant focus of today being the gift from God versus a future utopia in a foreign land.

Finally, Luciferians believe that knowledge of *all* things and skepticism are **good**. WHAT?!!!! Asking questions is a good thing? Why, yes, it is! Another difference for Christian-based thought is to never question God or to question its doctrine. They believe each person is also a summation of their personality and ability. Asking questions, figuring out your talent and abilities, and learning how to pivot is of utmost importance. It's what you *should* be doing with your time on earth. Use what you've got to get what you want, and don't be shy about it.

## What Luciferians do not believe

They do not worship Satan. Lucifer, also referred to as Satan in Christian doctrine, is not a bad character. He is a light bringer, a destroyer, and a guardian leading souls to darkness. The name Lucifer was just as common of a name as Joe or Dave. The Latin translation of Lucifer is "morning star." Luciferians see Lucifer as humanity's savior, encouraging enlightenment and independence and moving humankind to forward thinking.

## The Cornerstone of Luciferianism

Enlightenment and free will are the cornerstones of Luciferianism. Knowledge truly is power.

## Why Lucifer has been referred to as "the devil"

Because…confusion. The earliest Lucifer worshiper was revealed in 1231. From that time, Freemasons have been suggested to be the culprit behind the satanic agenda in its connection with Lucifer. The name Lucifer used in KJV text has been referred to as *Venus* or *The Morning*

*Star.* Over time, Christians have made *Lucifer*, *Satan,* and "the devil" the same person.

Neither Satan nor the devil are associated with Luciferianism. Luciferians do not believe in one person named Lucifer but in the broader sense of what the original angel represents as a lightworker, change agent, and enlightener. By this time, I'm all the way awake!

## Freemasonry and Luciferianism

Yep, the same folks that created the secretive fraternal order and the catalysts for the sororities and fraternities many Christians are members of today are connected to the Luciferian condemnation and perpetuation of false information. It is said that Freemason Albert Pike believed that Lucifer was God and that Adonai (the Hebrew God meaning "lord" or "master") was the opposition. This school of thought has been referred to as the "Taxil hoax," named after author Léo Taxil. Further, freemasons have contended that any reference to Lucifer was to the light bringer and morning star. Does this mean that Freemasons and Greek organizations like it are Luciferians?

## How they operate in 2024

There have been quite a few to carry the torch of revamping Luciferianism over generations. The most current thought leaders filed for "church" status in 2015.

**Space**

## Neo-Luciferianism Church (NLC)

The NLC is rooted in Western esotericism, Voodoo, Luciferianism, Thelema, and magic.

## Key takeaways for the reader

Lucifer is not Satan. Lucifer is a proper noun and common name. Satanism and Luciferianism are not the same. Lucifer is not the devil.

I believe that the intention behind the spirit handing me this word was to enlighten myself, as well as shed light on esoteric and its correlation to Christianity. It is fair to say that I could be considered a Luciferian. The exception is that I do believe, accept, and recognize the grace factor as offered through Jesus Christ as the base of my religion. Though, I do believe that if we all just choose not to be jerks, we don't need a God to tell us to do so. Self-regulation and community should be more than enough to hold us accountable if we are constantly seeking to do right by ourselves each day.

# Dear Black Jesus. This is my first wedding anniversary as a divorcee.

Today, my wedding anniversary feels different. I feel liberated. I feel free. I feel uninhibited from living life as God sees fit. I feel sad.

What went wrong in our marriage? Nothing. It went according to his plan most of the way. Then, once I enforced my own will in the areas that mattered most, the marriage ended. The end.

I'll probably never discuss our marriage in detail unless there's a hefty paycheck attached. Otherwise, it's just a story of two people who never belonged together but found ways to be together and raise a child together. Much of it is just like what everyone else is doing; coping and sticking together for the financial benefits.

I loved him deeply.

As we've both started our journeys outside of each other, I am excited for him to find **the one**. It was never me.

I used to love him.

Space

# Dear God, I'm starting to see "Mags" for who she was. Can you give her a new red lipstick for me?

I'm starting to learn that God will allow you to be in the presence of your enemies for your whole life. I'm also learning that he will cloak your energy and your essence to keep them from abusing you even more. Thank goodness for divine guidance, right?! I've never been one to fixate on being accepted. Sure, I've done some people-pleasing in my day. But, generally, I do whatever it is that feels right in my spirit…even when it hurts my feelings. This includes allowing myself to be the center of a lot of rumors and lies without addressing them. People are supposed to lie; that's just some people's destiny. My destiny is much more strategic, much more molecular, and much more revolutionary. I think we all have revolutionary work to do; some of us just don't have the faith to believe it yet.

Imagine being a woman who had one goal in mind…to please God. Imagine a woman who offered every shekel she could in order to play a background role in a work she'd never be center stage in. Imagine a woman, a beautiful woman, who would suffer the sweat, tears, and loss of her closest friend in order to ensure that history would have a savior so that history would have a *man* to revere. Imagine being called a whore, a dirty woman, the devil, a witch, a harlot, and every other word connected to a displaced chastity or moral compass and still being determined to show up for a friend. Imagine the embarrassment of being misunderstood.

Imagine the pain of family and friends choosing silence over devotion in your moments of hurt, judgment, and deep belief. Imagine being the last person people consider a "saint." Imagine being gorgeous and everyone using that against you just because they can. Imagine being confident in your femininity so much so that you gingerly reframe the

# Space

publicly accentuated negatives and have folks wanting to latch on to every affirmative associated with your God-given body and talent. Just…imagine being perfect, but no one wants to see it because you're a little odd and have a lot of mystery.

Mary Magdalene, said to be Jesus' twin flame, was all of the above. She knew how to put that "ish" on, as the kids say. She has been hailed as everything but what she really was…an apostle. Our patriarchal religious narratives have made her into just about every kind of sex worker you could imagine. They made her into every kind of demon known to man. The Catholic Church even had to admit that maybe they portrayed her to be much worse than she was. Consider TMZ retracting a statement thousands of years later to say that perhaps the hearsay about the biggest taboo celeb Vixen was from a source who couldn't keep his pants up. Or maybe the source "in her camp" was just jaded because she had turned him down on his violent sexual advances towards her. I'd be ticked off if I were her. I'd be sad to know the real story and no one ever believes mine.

I'd be sadder if I never attempted to tell my own story.

Known to be one of the devout, bossed-up women in the scripture to bankroll Jesus' crusade to tell the world about God, Mary Magdalene was the first to note that Jesus had risen. She was there for his life, death, and resurrection. She was there to wash his body in the tomb. She was there to make sure that all twelve of those disciples got to and fro with Jesus. She showed up when Judas was committing the ultimate sin for money. She was the only one to witness Jesus' resurrection and confirmation of his transformation to Glory. In John 20:17, Jesus calls His father her father. He calls His God her God. Only a beloved person could be given such a gift.

Only a true soldier of the gospel could witness such a miracle. It's no mistake that she is who Jesus revealed his new face, new body, and new spirit. **Mags was really that girl!**

Society has gotten it all twisted. Women are exploited daily by patriarchal systems and ideologies that do not affirm women. We have diminished women to sex and breasts. We have diminished women to dark witches and whores, simply because we don't understand them. Yet, we allow men to go on for decades violently raping, cowardly cheating, and misusing the divine feminine without batting an eye. We've even taught women to hate the very nature of themselves by encouraging them to fully cover themselves in an effort to suppress their power, all in the name of "modesty." We let women tear each other down in the comment section of internet conversations just because a woman has chosen to show midriff. Our mothers even tell us how undesirable we are simply because we choose to show up authentically as ourselves instead of cornering ourselves into self-imposed toxic and narcissistic environments that become the bedrock of what it is to be a woman.

We praise men with multiple children by multiple women in multiple states, countries, and jurisdictions. We allow those men to tell women who they *should* be. We allow those men to spread semen across state lines while carrying the very covenant of marriage that they often hide from the women that they bed, while later calling them whores. We allow women like Mary Magdalene to go on for centuries with a broken story. We allow hearsay to rule our minds while never uttering a word to restore the reputations of women who just happen to like who they are. It's no wonder Diddy, 45, Epstein, R. Kelly, Elvis, your uncle, your creepy cousin, and even that sick neighbor go on to live lives engulfed in stories of their own sick, demented, and fetishistic views on women. Those men rarely atone, rarely properly emote, and much more rarely see the error of their ways. We won't even talk about how much they rarely get help in the therapeutic form to heal their own bad behavior and dark realities. We just put a suit on them and called them pastors, military men, or "bosses" and act like they're Jesus the Christ (insert eye roll).

Mary Magdalene would likely be every bossed-up woman who has chosen to use her body to advance their personal success (think Iman, Melyssa Ford, Pamela Anderson, or…Melania Trump). A success that is driven by very lustful and judgmental men. Shame on us! What have we done?

# Space

What are we to tell history about the value we place on a woman's life? Women are being raped, impregnated, and told that they must carry the child because…"murder." Then we tell them we cannot help them care for the child because they are slightly above the poverty line. Those children grow up to be the epicenter of an impoverished nation. We also have men that choose to have consensual sex with women and then slut shame them for consenting to the very act that the man gains energy and favor.

That's right! Women bring favor to the male species. Women bring harmony in dissonance. The womb of a woman is the very portal to blessings. The touch of a woman is a balm. The essence of a woman ever lingers for generations and steers the ship of prosperity. Mags should be praised as we do: Mother Teresa, Michelle Obama, Oprah, Melinda Gates, Gloria Steinem, and every other boss's feminine energy encapsulated in the very thought of philanthropy.

If Mags did it, so will I. If she can withstand the wilds of public opinion, so can I. If she can seek his face and dedicate her life to doing the work of a father she'd never seen, so can I. If she can be called a whore, home wrecker, witch, evil spirit, and public enemy number one, so can I. If she can hold her peace and let her father fight her battles, so can I. If she can be herself and savor the favor of her beloved and God, the father, so can I. If she can have her name made great, so can I.

Long live Mags!

*Dedicated to every woman in my lineage who has been misunderstood for being who she is. To every woman who has never shared the bonds of matrimony because she has been subjected to being a third party. To every woman who has been exploited by the very ones charged with cherishing her divinity. To every woman that's been reduced to the mystery between her thighs. To every woman on the front lines of justice. To every woman that made it possible for me to live loudly. To every woman that made it cool to be weird. To every woman who holds a faith so deep in her bones while walking alone and blind.

Your honor has been restored.

# Leave it all behind

I keep coming back here to Iris Drive. My room is different. The whole house is. In my mind, I've left something I want. Not even something I need, just a want. For years, I've gone to bed only to return to this place and wonder why. Each time, I grow more and more frustrated by what I find. More stuff that I can't control. There's even an uglier bathroom rug. Man, she has poor taste! Daddy is there, all the time, in some other shape than the way I left him. I knew she'd kill him, and she did. One way or the other, she did. My soul knew it in 2012 and again in 2014, just days before he left.

But, I ain't asleep anymore. He's dead, and guess who isn't…

Today, in the dream, God told me to leave it all behind. Leave everyone behind. Where I must go requires solidarity and loyalty to myself, for once.

Let it all burn down. The phoenix is on its way…

# Chapter 4

# North Node

# For Powerhouse.

For almost a year, I have been on a wild goose chase with God. Not understanding the path before me. Not seeing the road, if there even was a road. Not knowing just what was coming at me. Feeling projections and wickedness, I've never felt before; I kept praying and walking by faith. Like a nightmare, I have relived things I never remembered seeing. I have cried the tears of a million saints. I have been in deep contemplation. I have no idea why He chose me. But now I know it's because I'm not afraid. I'm bold. I don't care enough to be swallowed by public opinion or a church lady's condemnation. My eyes are forever affixed on Him.

Between the curse words and spaghetti straps is a good woman. I was raised, and then I did the work to redirect the raising I got into purpose. My whole life, I have cared for "the least of them." Loyalty is so important to me, but rarely do I find people who are loyal to me, not like *Powerhouse.*

No one is loyal to anything like *Powerhouse* was loyal to my mother and father, the pastors of this church. *Greater Powerhouse of Deliverance*, the only church home I've ever had, is who I owe for raising me. All of my childhood was laced with the love of mothers, the care of brothers, and the siblings of others. I grew up there. I slept there, as most church kids do. I lived there. On the land that my grandmother purchased for my father, that hill was magical and a curse, all at the same time.

Like the *Ghost of Christmas Past*, God, my ancestors, and spirit guides have been taking me through scenarios that I didn't understand and didn't know without telling me WTF I was doing. Why me? Are the other five siblings going through this, too? Being the last of 6 children makes you question fairness often and fervently. LOL! We won't go into that, though. I just wanted to ensure that God 'knew that I was tired of life kicking my own behind. I did not want any more of anyone else's work. I see now that it was imperative for me to feel the pain of other people, to see what they endured, and to understand just how many people have **stayed** near the cross on my behalf.

My father was a cool dude. I'm learning, perhaps, too cool for school. Very complicated. But everyone is complicated. He struggled with being a hustler and being a man of the cloth. Sometimes, they blended together.

Sometimes, he forgot to lay the D.C./Memphis down and it came out in spaces it wasn't needed. Most times, he was everyone's favorite pastor. A highly intellectual and comical man, he made learning fun. He taught with a back of iron, unafraid, it seemed, of what he was teaching and unafraid to be asked any question at all. He is the teacher I aspire to be, only wiser. I have spent decades of education and research studying things that don't matter to me now. I got into law school easily. I got into a doctoral program easily. I've dropped out of both now. I realize the decision to take that journey was God-ordained, as well. Though, I realize, also, that I already have what I need to thrive. No more student loans are needed.

After a very public and embarrassing divorce, my father raised me. My mother went on to live her life. I can't blame her. She likes the lights and glitz. Being a single mother, a thing she had been before, was of no real interest to her. My father was the best person to raise me, though he did not do it alone. There were other people sharing the load. I'm eternally grateful for them. They, the faithful few that hung around after everyone else, got a clue and moved on. Those people are my family. I'm not sure how I would've survived without them. Literally. I went on to live my life and be a wife and they are all still there in the city that made and broke me.

In a dream last night, God showed me, what feels like, is the final piece of the journey about church. The crazy part? I've had this dream before. I don't think I was able to digest it when I had it the first time. But, this time, after months of purging and praying, I saw it differently. I felt it much more deeply. The revelation hit home like a Mack truck. They tried. They tried to protect me. I had only ever known the babysitters, nannies, and housekeepers of my church family until adulthood. I don't ever remember being in the care of strangers. My church family fed me when they ate.

They hugged me when they loved their own. They taught me the scriptures. They taught me hymns. They supported me. Of course, you have some rascals in every bunch that I wouldn't trust with a flip-flop. But, overwhelmingly, I had the love of family because I had *Powerhouse*. I've felt closer to them than I've felt to my biological family. Some of them know more about me than my mother does. I'm glad I had someone, though my home had been broken.

Some of the best musicians, teachers, preachers, and spokespersons have come from *Powerhouse*. They have gone on to make their own way for their own children and grandchildren, but I still have them to thank today. I feel that this piece is to be a very public and thorough "Thank You" from my spirit team, too. My grandmothers, thank you. My grandfathers, thank you. I can't imagine what you have endured, the questions you've been asked, and the miles you have traveled, all in the name of loyalty and faithfulness to God and my parents. I don't deserve your loyalty, but I'm glad to have had it. Some of the deepest bonds I've ever had have been with *Powerhouse*. Play cousins, friends, crushes, and more…all with and at *Powerhouse*.

Earnestine and Roy…and yes, in that order. Earnestine leads, and Roy holds the fort. They parented me when my parents were absent, too tired, or otherwise too busy. The Bishops never forgot about me. I'm the chef I am today because of Earnestine and Mother Forbis. I'm the mother I am today because Earnestine showed me what it was supposed to look like. I'm the human I am today because of Earnestine and Ruth. Both are spicy women with combinations of love, aspiration, and loyalty.

I realize now that my job is to put *Powerhouse* to rest. I'm supposed to say goodbye to the old things and welcome the new. The magical thing about *Powerhouse* was everyone was themselves. A place full of eccentric people with stories about faith and fellowship. A foundation of solid musical experience (see any choir member), performative dress (see Mearle), the best testimonies (see Sheila F. and Calvaughn), the best recipes (see Sheila M.), and deeply rooted love (see anyone from Powerhouse). If I were a pastor's wife, it would be for people like you. People who bravely weather many storms in pursuit of faith and family.

You all never got the shine you deserved. Please allow me. May God richly bless you all. I'm rooting for you, for real! Goodnight, *Powerhouse*.

Forever yours,

Toosie

**\*for all of my church cousins and all of the church cousins to all PKs. Thank you for sharing your family with us.\***

# Dear God, I forgive my molester. Can you?

I was molested very young. Actually, it was before I even began my first menstruation. In fact, once I stopped being molested, I started my period. Weird how nature takes its toll on the body, huh? The weirder part? I have never hated him. I don't know why I couldn't, but I didn't. The older I get, the more I feel sorry for him. The little girl in me just felt numb. The 39-year-old in me understands that he didn't intend to hurt me. He was hurt, himself. He wasn't loved properly, himself. He needed care, himself. I was a tool to gain the very thing he could not earn or achieve from his family and friends. He was othered. He was broken. From my understanding, he's been broken for most of his life.

The thing about trauma is that it seeps into your bones, your brain, your spirit, and then into your heart and wreaks havoc on who you are. It shortens the circuit to your brain. It dulls the knife. It adds rust to every conductor in the body. It makes you someone different. It stifles the breathing in who you are, rendering you to dust. He was a child when his own traumatic experiences started. No one explains things to kids in the 70s and 80s in a southern, religious, black family. Just take the crap and smile. He didn't have a fighting chance. He also had plenty of examples in his life to teach him bad behavior, as did I.

This doesn't absolve him from all responsibility. But I understand the brain so much better as an adult. I understand pain so much better as a trauma survivor. PTSD has played so many mind games in my life. It has caused me to see things in the darkness. It has caused me to cling to people who were just as sick or sicker than I was. It rushed me into therapy. After the panic attacks, the brief moments of agoraphobia, and the constant spiritual warfare, it almost took my breath away. But I made it out. Therapy, medication, mindfulness, prayer…you know the vibes by now. I rely on a magic combo of natural and spiritual.

Last night, in a dream, my abuser asked for forgiveness. He couldn't even gather the words to properly express himself, but I knew what he was saying. Every now and then, the Master's in Education helps me to see and understand people right where they are. I've probably diagnosed a dozen people in my mind just this summer alone. He was the same way I remembered him. Diffident and juvenile in effect. But I forgive him. **I forgive you.** Be free! Take up your bed and walk, and never commit this sin again! EVER!

I've been sexually abused so many times in my life I've lost count. I didn't even realize some things were considered rape until the *Me Too* movement came along. I realize that devaluing myself started at home. That made it so much easier for other people to do it and get away with it. That made it so much easier to emotionally tie myself to men who would abuse me. An arm snatch here, a slap there. A bruise, a tear, a psychologically abusive few years, everywhere. That *was* my life. It's not my life now. I've created a new narrative for myself. I'm much more powerful. I'm much wiser. I'm solid within myself. I dare a MF'r to try that *now*. Lol!

God, I forgive him. Can you?

**North Node**

# Dear God! So, are you saying

# I'll be single forever?

*If so, just say that…*

I never imagined that I'd be romantically alone in my life. I'm just a couple of months out of divorce (much longer out of the union), and I've accepted that my life's purpose might involve me being single for the rest of my life. Right now, I don't think I'm in love with the thought, but I accept it. Like most women, I've dealt with so much heartbreak in romantic situations that I am not looking forward to the vulnerability that being in love requires. I'm not looking forward to the disappointment that humans bring into the equation. I'm much less interested in being alone, though. I mean, I do like romance, and I haven't met a bearded black man who didn't make my eyes glitter a little.

Honestly, I don't think I trust anyone enough to commit to. My faith in humans is just…shotty. I know I'm not alone in this sentiment. I'm certain that people all across the globe feel me on this one. Truthfully, I don't think I've ever trusted anyone completely in my life. Is that bad to say out loud? I'll answer that. It sounds horrible! I was with a man for 22 years, and I should've been able to trust him. But I didn't. It's not entirely his fault. My Intuition tends to tell me things that I wish it didn't, sometimes. Sometimes, being a seer can feel like a curse. I KNOW it is not, though. And I am grateful that you chose me, God. I am. But I'm concerned.

As a former polyamorous person, I am clear that I do not want to be in that sort of love style in the future. There is something beautiful about love. I can't say my experience was all bad, really. In fact, it opened my mind in ways I would've never imagined. It, in essence, healed me of ailments I didn't know I had. Or maybe it turned the light on for me to see them so that *I* could fix them. Either way, I'm better for the experience. I'm better for the wonderful men and women that I met on that journey. I hope they are all excelling. But I know that I was intended to be a monogamous woman. I know that your design for my life requires peace in my nervous system—something I cannot get from dating in multiples. However, I know so many "monogamous and saved" couples who are living a secretly polyamorous life that I do not feel safe dating within the church either. Oddly enough, I've had better luck with thugs (insert smirky grin). They usually appreciate loyalty, and protecting and providing are often high on their list. But you have to keep your head on a swivel in those relationships, too. Ugh!

I guess what I'm saying is that I've accepted that my answer to your call means that I will likely traverse this path alone. Just you and I, God. And I ain't mad at it. Really, I've given up so many other things, so many other people, that I can survive working alone. Because I refuse to be anyone's third party, I refuse to play games. I refuse to offer up my divine energy to another person that isn't worth the spiritual exchange. And while I'm saying this, I do hope that you decide to send me THE guy for me (you know what I want). I won't be mad if he fits my list and exceeds my expectations. If you decide to do that, please ensure that I blow his mind, too. I'll dust off my best tricks for him (insert shy laugh and black girl blushing). I want him to pray for me, and I never feel preyed upon.

Answering the call to do your will has been conflicting. I understand my assignment. Well, as it stands today. You keep revealing parts of the road map that I didn't know were there. It's okay, though. I trust you, and I'm sticking to the plan. At 39, I don't think people are really checking for me like that, anyway. I mean, I'm not ugly or anything. I just think people are a little afraid of me. LOL! And I'll never consider anyone from my past again. I must've really been ill. For a moment there, I thought I had met THE ONE. I guess that was a big SIKE. He would've never been supportive of the work you've laid before me unless it came with a paycheck for him, which confirms that he was NOT the one. Then the other guy...he's too concerned with public opinion and unreliable. Revolutionary work cannot be done by such people. He definitely isn't the one, either.

I've purged everyone from life. I send everyone love and light, including my ex-husband. And I'm committed to doing what you've anointed me to do.

I'm ready for the path. My journey into this world was one filled with uncertainty and the path ahead is clearer than it's ever been. The path ahead is purer than it's ever been. I'm ready. For real. I am. If I have to be alone to do the work, let the angels and ancestors accompany me and guide the path. Give me the words to speak, and I shall. Keep leading me daily. Give me the health and strength to do your will.

For good measure, though… I'll put the list of characteristics of my perfect guy in a safe place. Is the cloud safe these days? I know your memory is good; I just want to be efficient. It's a short list; you know I'm easy to please. I know you know my dream guy is on my vision board already and has been for two years, but I don't know him yet, and I want to leave room for you to surprise me (insert spoiled child smile). Anoint us both for the work, should he come.

Still, I will go alone if it be your will.

# Hand, meet plow.

Brandi, the woman the world has known for 39 years, has left the scene. A ghost has entered the picture. I won't go into too many details, but I am shocking myself. I really am not my own (1 Corinthians 6:19–20). It's almost like *Freaky Friday,* and I woke up one day as an ancestor…one of the holy ones. Perhaps someone from my mother's side of the family. My father's side is much more…matter of fact. Less talk, more muscle. Though, I kinda think one of those ancestors entered the chat long ago. Still, life is a bit different for me now. I even think church men are kinda sexy now. Who would've thought? I saw this pastor online who was fly, bearded, and loc'd.

Ooohhweee!

My mind has been consumed by the work of The Lord. I'm still me, for the most part, but I never imagined I'd be *this* woman. I never imagined I'd be this open. I never imagined I'd be this…channel for God. It is the most satisfying thing I've been in life. Plaques, long resumes, and certifications to the side. I see the benefits of serving God in 2024. I see the value of telling God I'd go. I see the joy in giving God my time and commitment to correcting the ills of the past in my bloodline and generation.

For nearly one week, I have been on assignment all over Cleveland. I have been going about life doing things that I would normally do while being my country ass and talking to everyone. Almost every place I went, he led me to pray. Not under my voice or in my head, like I normally do, but out loud. Hands stretched and mouth open. I was always told to be careful of where you lay your hands. But when He told me to, I did. It was an honor to be his vessel.

The tears I have seen over the last seven days… The healing I have seen occurring in the spirit… The healing, I believe, is taking place… I told God I'd go, so here I am. I told God I'd speak, so here I am. I have listened closely to the words people have spilled from the depths of their souls in stores, salons, over the phone… It only reaffirmed my faith. It only made me fall deeper into worship.

The *Piano Lesson*, a movie now on *Netflix*, depicts the conjuring of the power of God and the ancestors of the character coming to their aid. The prayer shakes the home, breaks the glass, and unlocks their ancestors. As they appeared, the energy of the home was restored, and peace swept through. It was powerful. It was majestic. It was something I experienced in real life. It was the only depiction I've seen that properly describes what happened with my own spiritual experience. Well, at least one of them.

With my feet in the grass while grounding, I prayed fervently for help. After a heated conversation with my ex-husband one night, I walked into the grass to ground my energy. I asked him to join me, but he declined. No biggie. I stood there, after midnight, in my suburban neighborhood with wet grass beneath my feet during a cold night in Ohio. Exhausted with trying to salvage my marriage while healing the heartbreak from a different man and in the middle of my neighbor's property line, I begged God for help. I begged the ancestors. Crying and snotty, I begged. Desperate for help, I begged. "Grandma, pleeeeeeassse! Daddy, where are you?" I was no stranger to communing with God and my ancestors. I learned a while ago that they walk with me closely.

In an instant between one beg and the other, a swarm of energy came from both sides. No faces to see, just a blur. I saw it. I felt it. All of a sudden, "I want a divorce" flew from my mouth. "I'm serious this time. I want a divorce." Afterward, we went into a whirlwind of curse words and tears.

We moved into the house from the yard. While standing, knees knocking and stuttering, I protested for what I wanted. I don't know how I got the strength, but I know they were there. Since then, I have felt the strength of a million souls here and there. I stopped smoking weed that day. I knew I needed to clear my head. I worried about how I'd manage my pain, but my faith was much stronger than my ills. I went cold turkey, and then, on occasion, I micro-dosed.

# North Node

Always a dreamer, my dreams heightened. Messages started coming in clearer. I told God that He could have me. I told God I'd do the work. I had to continue healing myself first. Simultaneously, He sent me on assignment. He kept talking to me and giving me messages to share. I obeyed. I was mocked sometimes, but I kept going. God instructed me to keep my eyes on my own paper. Done. He instructed me to hike. Done. He instructed me to shut the door on people. Like a good Viola Davis scene in any movie where she's crying, I lamented with proper amounts of snot rolling from my nose. It hurt. I even tried giving deadlines to soften the blow. He didn't agree. I woke up one Saturday morning and then, "Times up"! The word came in crystal clear. Done.

I'm not my own anymore. A very hard thing for a control freak to surrender to and then admit. I have never known a faith like this. I have never known a peace like this, either. My senses heightened. It got easier for me to sniff out the craziness. Then, an attack that put me in jeopardy of losing custody of my child from a family member came in. It crushed me. It angered me. I gave it to God to handle — I had made a decision to stop fighting, especially my family. They believe in calling the police, and I'd already spent a night in jail for false claims (see my Patreon). I prayed, contacted a family member to mediate a conversation, and then closed the door on a relationship I never wanted anyway. I never looked back. I never will.

Yet, I told Him I'd go if He led me. He has led me all the way to this moment. He led me to this second. He anointed my hands, my voice, and my senses to do the work. He has anointed me for His will. He has anointed me to walk boldly throughout the earth, professing the power of His Spirit (Mark 16:15–16).

So, hand, meet, plow.

# Black, religious & on the DL

A message to the black & down low community

I'm worried about you. It's 2024, and I really think it's time we empower people to be who they are. But that's not always true for *you*. It is much more likely that some woman will find out her husband likes anal stimulation and will want to gtfo. And that really should not be because men *should* like anal stimulation. It's where their sweet spot is. Does that make them gay? I really don't think so. If a man desires romantic connections with men, *that* is something different. And I think saying that should be accepted by society.

Which is why I'm worried. Society doesn't accept that, and your inability to be who you are is causing recklessness, leading to the death of more women. The HIV/AIDS crisis being seen in black women in 2024 is scary. I fear this because there is an increase in the number of men who are on the DL. I think the fact that there are more openly gay men today has increased access for black men. However, it has not increased safety for the black gay community.

I wish people would get educated on sexual health if they are going to have sex of any kind in 2024 and beyond. There is NO way to know your health is good if you're not checking it. If you haven't had a sexual health exam with a complete STD/STI panel within the last 10 years, you should get one, regardless of your marital history. The truth is, people be having sex (which is healthy), and sometimes their partner could be into different things (which might not ensure your health is good). And honestly, it's 2024. There's no excuse not to know your status and manage it as closely as you monitor your sexual organs being intertwined with someone else's. And you should get an update every time you change partners. Trust no one but God and lab results with your sexual health.

Honestly, I think if men were able to discuss their desire for anal stimulation with their partners, there would be much less of an issue.

# North Node

There would also be a lot less cheating, too. Ultimately, a lot less people would be hurt in the process. People could actually make genuine connections with people. Overall, that could reduce the health risks we are seeing. We cannot wait for the government or big pharma to save us.

Let me be clear. I do not think prostate orgasms are bad. I do not think it should be a crime (even though it has been) in 2024. I am an advocate for better communication within marriages, sexual partnerships, and health professionals. You don't owe anyone else an explanation of your sexual preferences. They are yours until you decide to change them. Be set free!

I think this piece is to discuss ways in which we MUST communicate about sex more like the real sex. We should talk about the one all of our men desire because that's typically the sex you get, one way or another. Women tend to follow the lead of men in bed, responding to their desires. Women typically have to navigate our satisfaction around what men want. Sadly, men rarely discuss their truest desires with women. They always leave something out because they feel they'll be judged harshly. Women are used to being judged harshly. Men can't handle being judged. They lose their minds and become extremely homophobic or mean-tempered at women as though we are to blame for their inability to get what they desire. Everyone should be in charge of their own pleasure during sex. It should be a dance of each person giving something and taking something.

Religious DL community, I'm worried about your mental, emotional, spiritual, and sexual health. Please communicate your sexual health with every partner and have that same expectation from them, before you connect on an emotional or sexual level. Sex is not a bad thing, but hiding your sexual health and preferences from your partner(s) can be. Those discussions empower everyone involved. People should be able to choose whether they want to take a lifelong trip or a Lyft back home.

Pastors in the down-low community... It's time you sit down and seek God for direction. If you are struggling with your sexuality, it's best to step down and seek God. You are not ruined, but you need to take a breath, restore your soul, and then come back when you are stronger. I am temporarily standing in the gap for you until this message finds you. Be ye loosed!

Women, step into your highest self and assess whether it is more important to be alone or with a man that loves you, wants to take care of you, AND gets some anal stimulation from YOU during sex. Perhaps, compromise somewhere between an anal toy and self-stimulation (in case you cannot agree to be a part of the experience). It may not be as bad as you think. From years of emotional connections with men (most of whom I never mounted □), anal stimulation is something men want but are afraid to ask for. Biologically, it makes complete sense. God (or evolution) put the prostate where it is on purpose. So, let's not be obtuse in discussions around satisfaction and how it is to be gained during sexual exchanges between heteronormative partners. Take the stick out of your behind (or... □). It's long overdue for us to just let people enjoy healthy and balanced sexual exchanges.

Now, if you decide that you do not want to be with a man that is not attracted to men but enjoys anal stimulation, do yo thang, girl! I support that. This is simply about stimulation. If there is more to the desire surrounding sexual pleasure with another man, then that needs to be communicated, too. If both partners don't agree to engage, it is okay to separate in the kindest way.

Black community, church community, we MUST save ourselves. Churches, we need to start dialogue on it. I'll be waiting for your call... Be ye loosed!

John 13:34 — God loves humankind, and humankind shares that love with each other.

PB4

# The Mass Casualty of Jezebel

Sure. I'm a woman of many faces and have taken full advantage of my femininity in life. I am also smart, which poses a whole other threat to people. I cannot be swayed by simple chatter and gossip. There is more to me than hips, lips, and fingertips. I am also a highly spiritual woman. I am the daughter of a highly spiritual woman. I am the offspring of women who, in the belly of a ship, came to the US by force and conjured spirits of protection and wisdom in order to survive rape, death, and famine in a foreign land. I am the final child of a jolly and charismatic Southern preacher. I am the dark feminine in a room full of faux lighting. I am not totally soft in my approach to anything, especially when money is concerned.

And I am the daughter of Jezebel. I was born into power, control, and manipulation. I was groomed to trust no one and assert my dominance wherever I landed my feet. My life was choreographed to win and never play second best. I was shown how beauty and femininity could lead not only men but nations into war and victory. I've watched men lust and grovel to only touch the bodice covering of a curvy black woman. I know how to get what I want by using what I have between my thighs and my eyes. After all, it's within my DNA to make the world fall to its knees as I waltz into any room. I am the daughter of control.

Jezebel is not only in my DNA, it's in yours. The very idea of control and dominance lies within us all. In a country that proverbially pees across the seas and stakes its claim even where it shouldn't, I only know control. Who would choose to be controlled? Though, we all have been. Jezebel isn't the lusty young thing walking across city streets. She isn't the single mother of three that society condemns. Jezebel is at the helm of every great nation. She is the leader in most Christian churches. She is in every piece of religious propaganda and societal groupthink. Jezebel is the master of control. She is the mother in every family that hastily oversees who is allowed to be wed and bred into the lineage. She is even every victim of lack who has had to assert dominance and control in order to build boundaries and nets of safety due to a lack of security.

# North Node

We are all the children of Jezebel. In so many ways, we all seek to control our environments as a way to control our outcomes. We are other members of society in an effort to be a "cool kid". Sadly, the "cool kid" lofty goal never ends at puberty, it lingers into retirement age and reminds us to vote in only our best interest. We all struggle with manipulation. We all have twisted reality to fit our desired fate. And that is the work of Jezebel. Jezebel must die. Everyday.

Romans 12:2 reminds us that we are not to conform to the ways of the world. It reminds us that we have to push auto-refresh every day in order to defeat Jezebel. 1 Corinthians 15:31 reminds us that we can only achieve redemption by putting Jezebel to death, daily. Our ways of control must end.

## Church

It is not ordained by God to shame and condemn other religions. God's grace is evident through his death, burial and resurrection for all people. Dress code, tax bracket, and methodology should not be a part of our witness. Love is the witness. Therefore, we must kill the Jezebel that is within us.

## Work

It is not ordained by God to step on others in order to advance our careers and salary bands. Backroom career moves hurt everyone. Therefore, Jezebel must die.

## Lies

The creation and fostering of untruths are the very essence of Jezebel. 1 Kings 21 shows how Naboth was killed as a direct reflection of Jezebel's lies. Therefore, the Jezebel in us that causes us to lie and be deceitful is the very antithesis of God's loving mission. We must kill the Jezebel within us, daily.

# North Node

## Control

Like many of you, I have sought to control every aspect of my life. It was only until I started to kill Jezebel that I realized my unwillingness to allow God to take control of my life was my truest flaw. The more I controlled, the further and further away from His will I became. Once I started to seek only His way for my life did I move further into my highest self. The more I sought His will for my life, the more I attracted the things that I desired for my life. My success has been a direct reflection of my faith in God and His will for my life. To kill Jezebel, we must relinquish control. At the heart of Jezebel's essence is the desire for control. The church's inability to allow God's love to lead encourages Jezebel's growth. Hungrily, she seeks to destroy the hearts of men each week from a pulpit. She breathes fire across nations under the guise of religious freedom. God's grace is open to **everyone**. Any church unwilling to welcome everyone without prejudice is operating under the veil of Jezebel.

Jezebel MUST die!

We must kill her through prayer, supplication, and course correction. She lives in our bloodline. She lives in our ancestry. She lives in our greed for more power, more money and more control. Lest she die, we will not live through Christ.

PB4

# Load The 'Choppa

Words are powerful. I've made several videos on social media about how words are spells, what our tongue speaks, and what our minds think are the very engines of what our life becomes and how far we go in life. I'm learning that our mind is power-packed with energy, and every intention is a seed in how our garden grows. Generations upon generations have been carrying the burdens of the misled intentions of our ancestral lines. Like blood, the energy of those who have come before us is our life force. Unless there is disruption in the flow we will repeat the same mistakes of times past. We will carry the same blessings and burdens of our lineage unless we transfuse our bloodline with something new.

Imagine each thought, each intention, projection, and rumor we repeat is one .45 caliber bullet loaded into the chamber of our bloodline. Each sin the father commits and does not correct is passed down to another generation, and it could skip a generation or two. The greatest minds of any time could be lying dormant in your bloodline. What will they experience as a return of your actions? Each act of incest that is swept under a rug… one bullet. Each rape… two bullets. Each lie about who a child's real father is… 3 bullets. Each act in dark magic (think voodoo and freezer spells, for instance)… 6 bullets. Everything we don't atone for… 8 bullets. Each person's career that we derail… 10 bullets.

And then 30 years later… "tat…tat…tat…tat…tat!"

… it rains iron in the form of the same intentions you sent out. Incess continues and becomes so common that it is impossible to disprove. Financial illiteracy continues. Teenage pregnancy increases. Addictions in many forms take over your family and everyone connected to you. The problem with generational curses and karmic returns is that they always arrive at the worst possible time. It returns with interest. One white lie turns into a black abyss of hopelessness that carries for another 100 years.

# North Node

Similarly, good energy put into the ether returns in the form of precipitation of generational curses removed. Suddenly, you look up and people are going to therapy and healing their wounds. Generations upon generations improve professionally when seeds of good belief are planted. The 'choppa is loaded with the ammunition of soft rain and good soil, creating sustenance for generations to come. Load the 'choppa with goodness. Remove the 50-year-old bloody bandages and replace them with healing salves. Open your ears to hear the truths that may be uncomfortable and full of lamentation. Unload the trauma at the kitchen table, on FaceTime at the reunion, and get down to cleaning the chambers of our bloodlines.

$2+0+2+5=9$

As we enter the year of "9", let us start to assess our wounds. Allow people to heal their crises with identity. Welcome the prodigal sons home, judgement free. Cook your healthiest calves for the celebration and show what course correction looks like. 9, meaning the end of a cycle. 9, meaning higher consciousness. 9, meaning the possibility of new things to come.

The gun will be loaded, but with what? That is up to you and I to decide.

PB4

www.ingramcontent.com/pod-product-compliance
Lightning Source LLC
Chambersburg PA
CBHW061715120626

46550CB00003B/1235